PRIMARY LANGUAGE C[OURSE]

WRITING LEVEL 1   BARBARA BENSON

Contents (or topics in this book)

Up the street   pages 2 and 3
Houses and homes   pages 4 and 5
Families and friends   pages 6 and 7
Animal families   pages 8 and 9
Names for people   page 10
Names for animals   page 11
Names for things   page 12
Who am I?   page 13
An ordinary day   page 14
A different day   page 15
House poems   pages 16 and 17
Days of the week   page 18
Birthday months   page 19
Presents   page 20
A party menu   page 21
Recipes nice and nasty   pages 22 and 23
Parties are fun   page 24
Parties aren't always fun   page 25
Birthday treats   page 26
Beautiful balloon trips   page 27
Helping hands   page 28
Help   page 29
A school assembly   pages 30 and 31
For the teacher   page 32

UP THE STREET

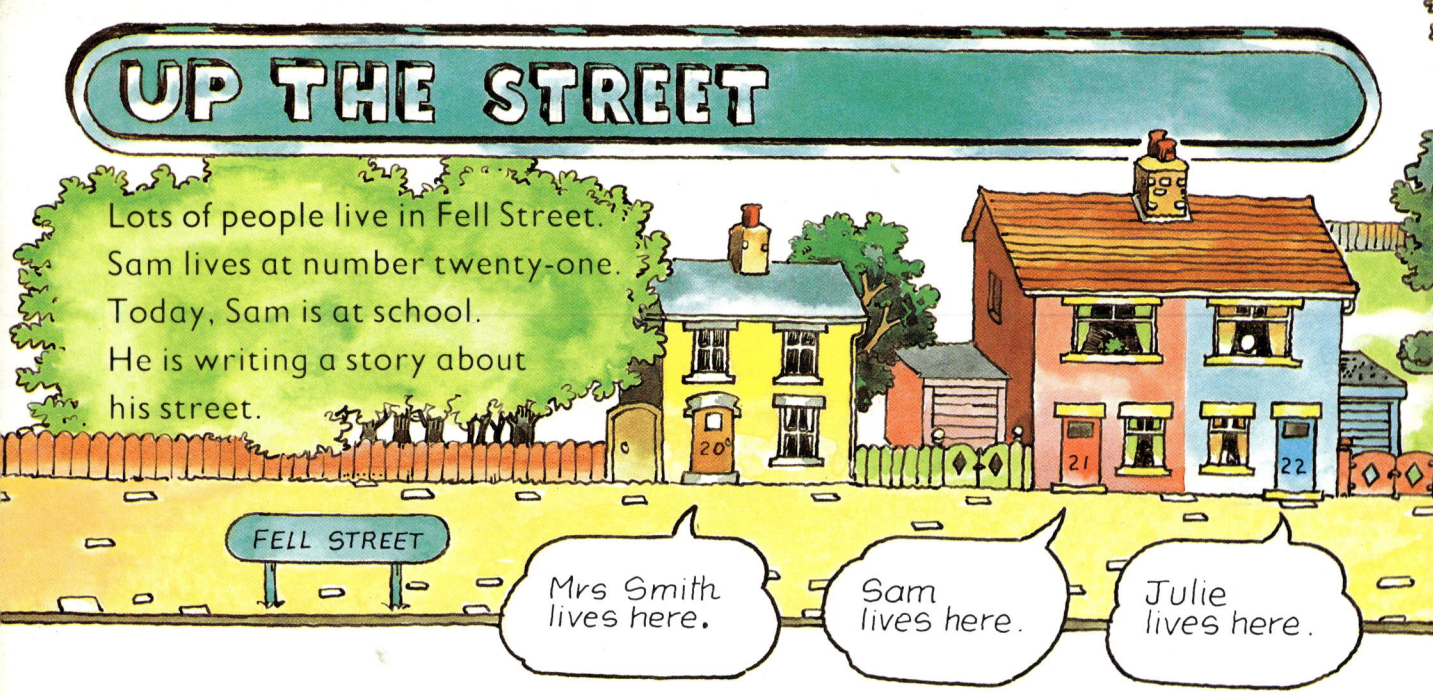

Here is Sam's story. Some words are missing.
Without these words, the story doesn't make
sense. Can you find the missing words?
They are all somewhere on pages 2 and 3.
The picture of Fell Street should help.

My street by Sam
I live in......street. Our house is number.....
My friend..... lives next door. We go to the same
..... Mr and Mrs..... live at the other side of
Julie. Sometimes we take their..... for a walk.
He is called..... I often go to the corner.....
for my Mum. Kama and..... live there.
They go to my..... as well. After school,
we often go to play in the.....

Now do this

Write out Sam's story, and put in the missing
words, so that the story makes sense.

Julie is also at school. She is writing about Fell Street. She describes how she goes to play in the park. Julie's story begins:

I come out of my front door. Then I turn left. I go past the ....

Things to do

1. Go on writing Julie's story.
   Does Julie call for a friend on the way to the park? How does she cross the road? What does Julie do when she gets to the park?

2. Draw a picture of **your** street. Don't forget to put the number on your door, if it has a number.

3. Write a story about **your** street. Describe the people who live there. The dog has some questions to help you.

Houses and Homes

Not everyone lives in a house.
Not everyone lives in a street.
But most people have a home somewhere.
It may be very large,
or very small.
It may be high up,
or low down.
It may be a busy place,
or a lonely place.
It may be on land,
or on water.

Look at the pictures on pages 4 and 5. You will see that homes come in all shapes and sizes.

Now do this

Make a list of lots of different sorts of homes.
You may need some books to help with this work.

Where would you like to live? Perhaps you can talk to your friends or your teacher about different sorts of homes.

Now do these

1 Pretend you have a new home. Draw a picture of it. The new home should look very different from your real one!

2 Write a sentence beginning
   My new home is a ....
Go on with the story about life in your new home. Here are some questions to help.
   What does it look like?
   What is it made of?
   Is it comfortable inside? Or is it uncomfortable?
   Does it stay still, or move about?
   Do you miss your old home?

FAMILIES AND FRIENDS

Today, Sam is with his family.
Look at these endings of sentences. They are all about Sam's family. Without their beginnings, the words in the sentences don't make sense.

.... is playing with the baby.
.... can't walk yet.
.... is playing tennis.
.... is having a cup of coffee.
.... is reading a book.

Sam's sister
Baby
Mum
Dad

Now do these

1 Find the right words for the beginning of the sentences. The picture will help.

2 Draw a picture of **your** family. Don't forget to put yourself in the picture!

3 Write some sentences about your family.

REMEMBER –
A sentence is a group of words which make sense.
A sentence starts with a capital letter.
Most sentences end with a full stop.

Look at this sentence.

> Most people have a friend.

Here are some beginnings of sentences about friends. Without their endings, the words in the sentences don't make sense.

> The seven dwarfs have a friend called ……… .
> Andy plays football with his ……… .
> Tom's best friend is the ship's ……… .
> It is lonely if you haven't got a ……… .

Now do these

1 Find the endings, and write out the sentences so that they make sense. The pictures will help.

2 Draw or paint a picture of **your** friend. It can be a real friend, or a pretend friend.

3 Write some sentences about your friend. Say why you like your friend. Describe some of the things you do together.

ANIMAL · FAMILIES

Animals often live in families. Baby animals have to be cared for, just like human babies. Their parents feed them, keep them clean, and protect them from enemies.

Here are the names of some animals and their babies.

dogs   kittens   foals   calves   cats
cows   lambs   cubs   sheep
frogs   chicks   hares
hens   puppies   joeys   horses
kangaroos   kids   lions
foxes   tadpoles leverets   goats

Now do this

Can you match the animals and their babies? Write in sentences, so that your answers make sense. Here is one answer to help you.

  Baby dogs are called puppies.

You should have twelve sentences altogether. **Two** baby animals have the same name.

Animal families, like human families, are not all the same. Some animals have lots of babies. Some have only one baby. Some baby animals are cared for in large groups. Some are cared for by just one parent.

Here is a father penguin. He is keeping the egg warm. He looks after the egg during the long cold winter months. When it hatches, the mother penguin brings food for her chick from the sea.

Here is a mother hedgehog. She brings up her babies on her own. If the father hedgehog comes near, she chases him away!

Now do this

Choose one animal family. Write some sentences about it. Explain how the baby animals are cared for. You may need some books to help you.

NAMES FOR PEOPLE

Here is Snow White with her friends, the seven dwarfs. Snow White has a pretty name. It tells us something about her. The seven dwarfs have names which tell us something about them.

Snoozy Crosspatch Cheerful Slowcoach Timid Snow White Prof Wheezy

Everyone has a name. Some people like their names. Other people don't like their names. If 'Crosspatch' had a different name, perhaps he wouldn't look so angry in the picture.

Things to do

1. Write down **your** name, and have a good look at it. Would you like it to be different? Pretend you have a new name. Write it down underneath your old name.

2. Draw a picture of yourself with your new name. Do you have some new clothes on, to go with it? Perhaps you look older, more grown up. Perhaps you are someone very important, or brave, or beautiful.

3. Now write a story about how you feel with the new name. Begin your story

   My new name is ……..

REMEMBER
The names of people begin with capital letters —
Snow White.

Names for Animals

The animals who live with us are called pets. They often have names. Dogs and cats know their names, and come when we call them. Horses have names. So have parrots, and even goldfish.

Things to do

1. Have you got any pets at home? If you have, write down their names in sentences, like this
       We have a dog called ....
    If you have no pets at home, would you like some? You could make up names for them.
       I would like a dog called ....

2. Think of some good names for these wild animals. Each name should tell us something about the animal.

    | I am a leopard called .... | I am a porcupine called .... |
    | I am a mouse called .... | I am an elephant called .... |
    | I am a spider called .... | I am a snake called .... |

    Here is one sentence to start you off
       I am a leopard called Prowler.

3. Now think of some more animals, and give them good names.

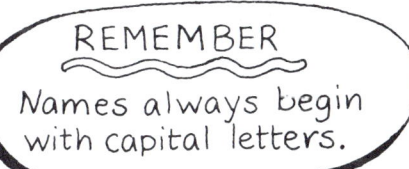

REMEMBER
Names always begin with capital letters.

NAMES FOR THINGS

People have names, but so do things. Otherwise, we should spend our time saying 'Pass me the thingamijig, please'. No one would know what we meant. Things in the kitchen have different names from things in the bedroom. Things in the park have different names from things at school.

Here is the beginning of a story told by a 'thing'.

> I am a dustbin. People put their rubbish in me. I am a round shape, with a lid on top. I live outside the house, near the back door. They put all sorts of things in me, tin cans, cornflake packets, teabags. I get very full sometimes ....

Things to do

1 Pretend you are a 'thing'. You can be something in the house, or at school, or on the beach, or anywhere. Draw a picture of the 'thing'.

2 Write a story about your life as the 'thing'. Begin your story

   I am a ...

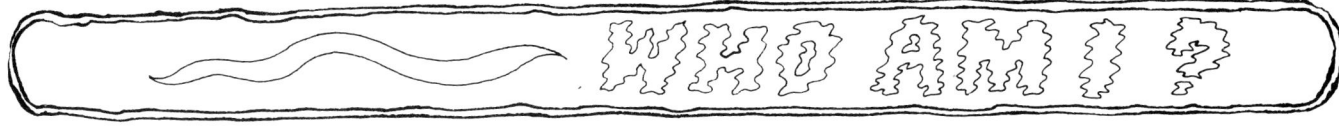

WHO AM I?

Here is a very puzzling question.

Who lives in the cave?

It may be a person, or an animal. It may be a monster or a ghost. It may be very fierce, or very timid. It may be someone strange, or something magic.

Things to do

1. Here is the beginning of a story about the cave. Write out the story, and put in the missing words. This time, you have to think of the missing words. They are not on this page, or anywhere else in the book.

    Once upon a time there was a .... who lived all alone in a cave. It was dark and cold in the cave, and the .... often felt sad. One day, the .... noticed someone coming towards the cave. Was it a friend or an enemy?

2. What happens next? Go on with the story.

3. Draw or paint a picture to go with your story.

Most sentences end with a full stop. But a few sentences have this mark at the end ? It's called a question mark. It means that the sentence is asking a question.

AN ORDINARY DAY

Can you tell the time? Look at the clocks in the pictures, and see if you can tell the different times.

Now do these

1 Read these parts of sentences about an ordinary day, when you go to school.

> I get up at ....
> School starts at ....
> At .... we have our dinner.
> My favourite subject is ....
> Afternoon school starts at ....
> We finish school at ....
> At .... we have our tea.
> My favourite television programme is ....
> It starts at .... It lasts for .... minutes.
> At .... I go to bed.

2 Write out the sentences. Put in the missing times, and any other missing words. When you have finished, you will have written a story about a schoolday.

3 Now write some sentences about a day at the weekend, when you don't have to go to school. Don't forget to put in the times.

4 Draw or paint two pictures of yourself, one on a schoolday, and one at the weekend.

Words you may need

o'clock   half past
quarter past
quarter to
morning   afternoon
night   evening

A DIFFERENT DAY

Sometimes, someone has a different sort of day. When Jack woke up in the morning, he looked out of the window and saw that a huge beanstalk had grown up in the night.

Things to do

1. Write a story about a different sort of day. Begin your story:

    One morning, when I woke up, everything felt different. I looked out of the window and saw ....

    You can choose anything for your story **except** a beanstalk! There can be lots of magic in the story, if you want.

2. Draw or paint a picture to go with your story.

HOUSE POEMS

A poem

Animals' houses

Of animals' houses
Two sorts are found,
Those which are square ones,
And those which are round.

Square is a hen-house,
A kennel, a sty,
Cows have square houses,
And so have I.

A snail's shell is curly,
A bird's nest is round;
Rabbits have twisty burrows
Underground.

But the fish in the bowl,
And the fish in the sea,
Their houses are round
As a house can be.

James Reeves

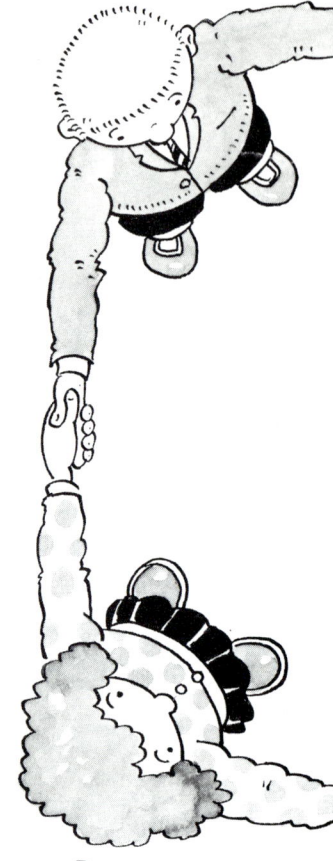

Have another look at the poem. A poem **looks** different from ordinary writing. The lines are shorter. They are set out on the page in groups. Each of these groups of lines is called a verse. How many verses are there in 'Animals' houses'? How many lines are there in each verse?

Now say the poem to yourself. A poem **sounds** different from ordinary writing. Some of the lines end in words with the same sound. These are called rhyming words. Can you hear the rhymes?

Now do these

1. Find the rhyming words in the poem 'Animals' houses'. Write them down in pairs. Here is the first pair

    found – round

2. Read these two lists of words. Find the rhyming words, and write them down in pairs.

    | sand | again |
    | sea | blow |
    | cloud | mountain |
    | snow | me |
    | rain | mouse |
    | fountain | crowd |
    | house | land |

     cloud – crowd

3. Now make a list of some more pairs of rhyming words.

4. Write your own poem about a house. It can be a real house, or a magic house. It can be a tiny cottage, or a huge castle.
   The poem can have lots of rhymes, or just one or two. It can have lots of verses, or just one verse if you like. Poems, like houses, come in all shapes and sizes.

REMEMBER
A poem looks different, and sounds different, from ordinary writing.

DAYS OF THE WEEK

Henry the Hippo collects tee-shirts. He has seven, one for each day of the week. When Henry's Mum washes them, the days always get mixed up. Can you sort out the tee-shirts, and put the days in the proper order? Start with Monday. Don't forget the capital letter 'M', because it's the name of a day.

Sam got a diary for Christmas. Each night, he writes one or two sentences in the diary about his day.

Now do this

Keep a diary for one week. Try to think of something different to write for each of the seven days.

Wednesday
We got up late Mum spilt the milk and Dad burnt the toast I just got to school in time.

Thursday
We had football this afternoon. Raju scored a goal, and I nearly got one.

Friday
It was my favourite school dinner today, sausages, beans and chips. I'm glad it's the weekend tomorrow.

Birthday months

Thirty days hath September,
April, June and November.
All the rest have thirty-one,
Excepting February alone.

Do you know the date of your birthday? You need to know the number and the month. A calendar will tell you which day your birthday is on this year.

Julie's birthday is on the 8th of December. Can you tell from the calendar which day it will be?

DECEMBER

Monday		6	13	20	27
Tuesday		7	14	21	28
Wednesday	1	8	15	22	29
Thursday	2	9	16	23	30
Friday	3	10	17	24	31
Saturday	4	11	18	25	
Sunday	5	12	19	26	

Now do these

1 Draw a picture of **your** birthday month. Is it a cold month or a warm month? Try to show in the picture what time of year it is.

2 Look at a calendar, and then write some sentences about your next birthday. What month is it in? What day will it be? Don't forget to say how old you will be on your next birthday!

REMEMBER
The name of each month begins with a capital letter.

Presents

One of the best things about birthdays is the presents.

Things to do

1. What would you like for your next birthday? Choose just one thing. Write a sentence
   For my next birthday, I would like ....

2. Now choose some presents for other people. Choose things which will make them happy. The presents can be for people in your family, for your pets, or for your friend. Make a list, like this
   Rex – a big bone

3. Choose a good present for **three** of these
   - a witch
   - a train driver
   - someone from space
   - a dragon
   - a soldier
   - a princess
   - a dinosaur
   - a mouse
   - a giant
   - someone alone in a cave

4. Write a story about how you gave a birthday present to **one** of the three people or animals. You had quite an adventure getting your present to them.

Don't forget to say in your story what the present was!

A party menu

A day or two before the 8th of December, Julie helped her Mum to get the food sorted out for the party. First, she asked her friends what they would like to eat. Here is what they chose.

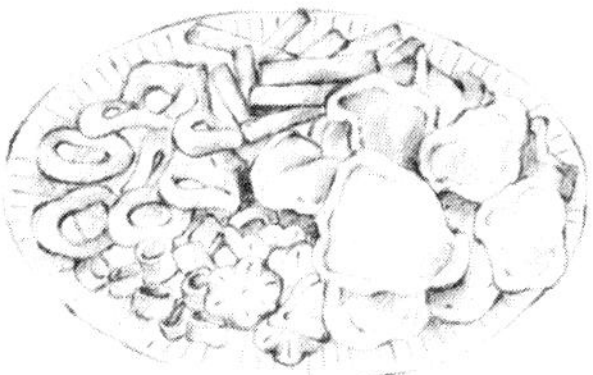

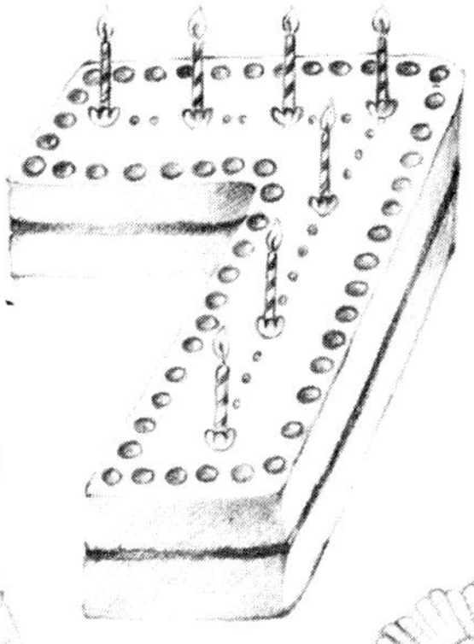

Raju curry pasties

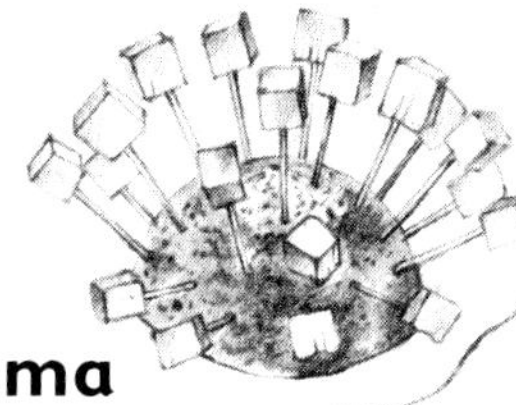

Penny sausage rolls

Sam ham sandwiches

Andrea birthday cake

Lisa crisps

Kama pineapple chunks

Emma trifle

Jonathan jelly and ice-cream

Things to do

Make out the menu for Julie's party. Think what you would eat first, then second, and so on. What should come last?

You can decorate your menu with a border pattern, to make it look attractive, if you want.

 Use a ruler to draw the border.

Recipes nice and nasty

Julie made some toffee crunch for her birthday. Here is the recipe, which tells you how to make it.

The ingredients (or what to put in)

100 grams of butter or margarine
One packet of marshmallows (about 100 grams)
One small slab of plain toffee (80–100 grams)
100 grams of Rice Krispies.

The instructions (or how to make it)

1. Put everything except the Rice Krispies into a large saucepan. (The toffee should be broken into pieces.)

2. Stir with a wooden spoon, on a very low heat.

3. When everything has melted and mixed together add about half of the Rice Krispies.

4. Take the saucepan off the cooker, and stir in the rest of the Rice Krispies.

5. Empty the mixture into a large flat tin (a meat tin or swiss roll tin will do).
Note: Grease the tin first.

HANDY HINT

Julie's Mum always helps her to make toffee crunch, because the saucepan is heavy and the mixture gets **HOT**.

Remember
Three important words

1. recipe
2. ingredients
3. instructions

Things to do

Write down your favourite recipe. You may need someone at home to help you.
Perhaps your teacher will let you try out some of the recipes at school.

Now do these

1. Not all recipes are for nice food.

   Can you think of a really nasty recipe?
   It can be as horrible as you like. Write down
   a list of ingredients and give the instructions for making it.

   Someone eats your horrible food.
   Write a story about what happens to them.

Parties are fun

Julie made a programme for her birthday party. In the programme was a list of party games.

Donkey's tail	Musical chairs
Pass the parcel	Hide and seek
Blind man's buff	Statues
I spy	Hunt the slipper

What is your favourite game? It may not be on Julie's list. It may not be a party game.

Now do these

1. Write some rules for your favourite game. These questions will help.

    Do you play the game inside the house, or outside?
    Do you need a ball to play your game?
    Do you need any other things, such as skipping ropes, bats, marbles, dice, chalk?
    How many people do you need to play the game?

2. Draw a picture of yourself (and your friends, if you like) playing your favourite game.

Remember Write in sentences so that the rules make sense.

PARTIES AREN'T ALWAYS FUN

Even parties have their ups and downs.
Some people aren't very good at party games.
Some people never seem to win. Sometimes,
someone cries, or feels sick, or wants to go home.

Sometimes, somebody turns up at a party who
hasn't been invited. If that somebody is
a witch, a monster, or someone from space,
strange things can happen. Magic things ....

Pretend you are at a party. Everyone is having
a good time. Then, suddenly

FLASH

AGH!

There stands a stranger, an uninvited guest.
Who is it?
What happens?
How does the party end?

Ooooooooh!

BANG

Now do these

1   Write a story called

    The party which went wrong

2   Draw or paint a picture of the uninvited guest.

BIRTHDAY TREATS

Sometimes, instead of giving a party, people invite their friends to share a birthday treat. They may go to a pantomime or the cinema. They may visit a leisure centre or the swimming baths. They may go to the zoo, to a safari park, or to the circus. Or ..... they may go on a 'trip'.

Can you choose somewhere for you and your friends to go on a special birthday trip? Here are some ideas to help you.

A trip to a huge sweet factory.
A sea trip to Rocky Point lighthouse.
A day up the beanstalk with Jack.
A rocket trip to the moon,
or to another planet.
A visit to explore an underground cave.

Now do this

When you have thought about it, write a story called **Our fantastic birthday trip**

Beautiful balloon trips

Up, up and away
In our beautiful balloon ....

Would you like to go for a
special trip in a ballon?
Who would you choose to go with you?
What would you see when you were
up in the sky?
What would it feel like?
Would you be glad to come down?

Now do these

1. You can choose **five** people to go with you on the balloon trip. Make a list of people to invite. They can be real friends, or pretend friends, or famous people you admire.

2. Write a poem called **The great big balloon**

   If you like, you can begin your poem with the two lines at the top of this page. Here are some pairs of rhyming words to help.

away	– day	air	– stare
trip	– slip	trees	– breeze
balloon	– soon	sea	– be
sky	– fly	stop	– drop

H·E·L·P·I·N·G H·A·N·D·S

First do this

Draw round your hand. Now think of lots of words for things you can do with hands. Write the words inside the hand.

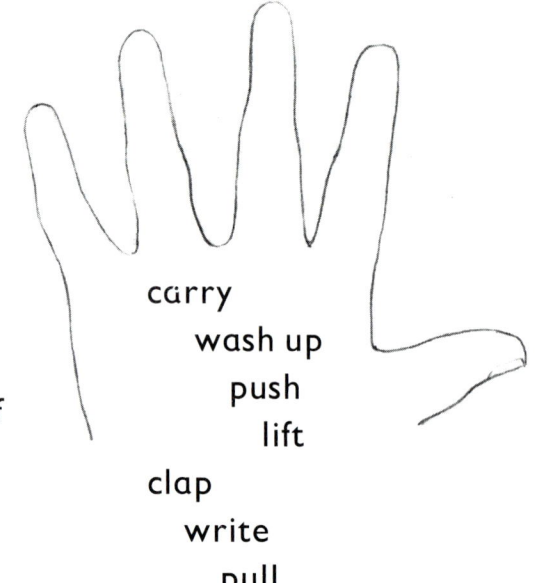

Look at the words inside your hand. Some of the words will be about things you can do to help.

Now do these

1 Here are some sentences about Sam. Some words are missing. They are all words about helping at home. Write out the sentences, and put in the missing words, so that they make sense. This time, **you** have to guess what the missing words are.

   Sam .... his bed.
   Sam .... the dishes.
   Sam .... his shoes.
   Sam .... the table for tea.
   Sam .... the path.

2 Write some sentences about things you can do to help in your home.

3 Draw a picture of yourself helping someone.

HELP

Some of our favourite stories are about people or animals who are in trouble. These stories usually have happy endings, because a kind person (or animal) comes along to help . . . like

Cinderella's fairy godmother.

Dick Whittington's cat.

The birds in Hansel and Gretel.

Things to do

1 Make a list of stories about helping. They can be true stories, or fairy stories. You will need lots of books to help.

2 Pretend that you are someone in trouble, and write a story about it. You can be yourself, or somebody else. You can even be a 'thing'. But you need help.
Ask yourself these questions first.

>Who am I?
>What sort of trouble am I in?
>Am I in danger?
>Have I got some enemies?
>Who comes to help me?
>How do they help?
>How can I thank them for helping me?

Let's hope your story has a happy ending!

A School Assembly

Now you are coming to the end of this book. It's time to plan your special school assembly. This is going to be the work of your class, with the help of your teacher.

What do you need for an assembly? Here is a list to help you.

1	Some of your own stories.	4	A short play.
2	Some songs to go with the stories.	5	Some poems.
3	Some pictures and paintings to go with the stories.		

Your assembly doesn't have to include all these things, but the list should give you some ideas.

1 Stories

Start with the stories. By now, you will have written lots of stories. You can choose stories from one of these ten topics, which are all in this book.

Houses and homes	Names	Fantastic trips
Families	A special day	Helping
Friends	A special time	
Animal families	Presents	

2 Songs

When you have chosen a topic (or two topics which go together), find some songs to go with it. Some of you may be able to play instruments, to accompany the songs. Make a list of songs, and decide which ones to have. Perhaps you could take a vote, to find the songs people like best.

3 Pictures and paintings

Can you decorate the school hall (or part of it) to go with your topic? You may have pictures, a frieze, or a model.

4 A play

If your class enjoys acting, it might be fun to turn one of the stories (either your own, or one from a book) into a short play.

5 Some poems

Find some poems to go with your topic. Some of you may want to read your own poems.

The programme

When you have worked out your assembly, and chosen all the things in it, make a proper programme. Ask your teacher to choose someone to read out the programme during the assembly.

Do you remember the decorated menu on page 21? Some of you can copy out the programme and decorate it, making enough copies for each class to have one. Remember to give the titles of the stories, songs and poems, and to say who has written them.

Don't forget to give a copy of the programme to your Head Teacher.   And **good luck!**

Good luck!

For the teacher

The grid below charts the links (either of topic or skill development) between this *Writing Book* and other materials at Level 1 in the Cambridge Primary Language Course.

Some of the *Talking and Listening* cards for Levels 1 and 2 will provide starting points for written activities in this book. *Word Play* Level 1 has more work on writing sentences, the use of capital letters, full stops and question marks. It develops in more detail nouns, verbs and sequencing skills. There are also more poems and rhyming words in *Word Play* 1. Certain skills developed in *Study Skills* Level 1 can be covered in conjunction with or as a follow up to work in this *Writing Book*.

Writing Book	*Talking and Listening* Card (title)	*Word Play* Level 1 (page numbers)	*Study Skills* Level 1 (page numbers)
Up the Street			
Houses and homes	Moving house, Homes		pp. 4 and 5
Families and friends	Families		pp. 2 and 3, 6 and 7
Animal families			
Names for people		pp. 20, 28 and 29	
Names for animals	Pets	pp. 12 and 13, 20	p. 15
Names for things		pp. 8 and 9, 28	
Who am I?		pp. 14 and 15	
An ordinary day	Time		
A different day			
House poems		see esp. 'mini poems' p. 27	
Days of the week		p. 28	
Birthday months		p. 28	
Presents	Surprise parcel	p. 26	
A party menu	Hungry?		
Recipes nice and nasty	How is it made?	p. 22	
Parties are fun	Games to play		
Parties aren't always fun			
Birthday treats		pp. 30 and 31	
Helping hands	Families	pp. 18 and 19	
Help!			pp. 12 and 13 (using book titles)
A school assembly	School fairs		

The author and publisher are grateful to the following for their valuable contribution to the book:
Rowan Barnes-Murphy, pages 4, 5, 12, 13, 14, 15 and the cover; Colin King, pages 2, 3, 22 and 23; Gwyneth Jones, pages 6, 7, 24, 25 and 28; Robin Lawrie, pages 10, 16, 17, 20, 26, 27, 29 and 31; Jenny Palmer for hand-lettering topic headings; Nicola Spoor, pages 3, 9, 18, 19 and 21; Rodney Williams, page 11.
The poem 'Animals' houses' © James Reeves is reprinted by permission of William Heinemann Limited.

Consultant Editor: John Hodgson

Published by the Press Syndicate of the University of Cambridge
The Pitt Building, Trumpington Street, Cambridge CB2 1RP
32 East 57th Street, New York, NY 10022, USA
296 Beaconsfield Parade, Middle Park, Melbourne 3206, Australia

© Cambridge University Press 1984

First published 1984

Printed in Great Britain
by Blantyre Printing & Binding Ltd.,
Glasgow and London.

ISBN 0 521 27067 7

KY

Contents

Chapter 1 — **Dressing up** — 4

Chapter 2 — **Historical Costumes**
  Costumes long ago — 6
  Costumes through the ages — 8

Chapter 3 — **Around the World** — 10

Chapter 4 — **Stage Costumes**
  Pantomime and circus — 14
  Ballet costumes — 16
  Television and film costumes — 18

Chapter 5 — **Famous Costumes** — 20

Chapter 6 — **The Make-Up Artist** — 22

Chapter 7 — **Masks and Props** — 24

Chapter 8 — **Making Costumes**
  How to make a clown outfit — 26
  How to make a pantomime cat — 28

Glossary — 30
Books to read — 30
Index — 31

Chapter 1

Dressing Up

Costume has always played a very important part in theatre. Since early times, people have dressed up using different ideas and materials to make themselves look like other people. Children often dress up to make-believe they are monsters, astronauts, doctors, nurses and other characters.

Have you ever thought why actors and actresses wear costumes, masks and make-up? Theatrical costume helps the actor become the part he or she is playing. It can tell the audience just by appearance if the character is old, young, rich or poor. Apart from suiting the character, a costume must also match the **set** and go well with other costumes. Colour is important in setting the mood of a scene — evil characters often wear dark clothes and a noisy or funny character might dress in bright, **vivid** colours.

When making costumes for a theatre, film or television production, there are many questions that have to be asked by the

Above This pantomime actor has used white face make-up and red eye-pencil to make himself look evil and sinister.

Left This scarlet and white devil's costume and mask looks extremely realistic.

costume designer. In which period of time will the production be set? Will it be in modern or **period costume**? In which country will it take place? When the costume designer is satisfied that he or she has enough information the plans begin. Books, paintings, postcards, magazines and museums will assist in making the designs. Meetings must also be held with the **producer**, set designer and actors and actresses to make sure that they are all in agreement about the costumes.

Masks and make-up can change an actor or actress's face. A mask gives a performer a fixed **expression**, so the audience will expect their character not to change. It could be very confusing for an audience if an angry-looking character turned out to be kind, after all.

Right Some of the many different characters played by actor James Cagney.

Below A happy and a sad mask used in Japanese theatre.

Chapter 2
Historical Costumes

Costumes long ago

People have been dressing up for more than 2000 years. **Prehistoric** cave paintings show that early men and women dressed up to disguise themselves. When they hunted for food they would try to make themselves look like the particular animal by wearing animal skins. The whole village would join in special dances which were a type of theatre. Masks were carved from wood and real antlers and horns were used to make the costumes look more **realistic**.

Ancient Greek vases tell historical stories in a series of pictures. The ancient Greeks used to dress up as larger than life characters, wearing huge, high-soled boots called *cothurnus* to make them up to 2m tall. The costumes would also be padded out so as the actor would not look unbalanced. To the ancient Greeks, the taller the actor, the more important the character. The Greeks also used very striking

Above A selection of masks used in ancient Greek theatre. Pick out which masks are sad, angry or happy.

Left An illustration showing ice-age people dressed in animal skins to hunt a mammoth – a large elephant-like creature which no longer exists.

Left An ancient Greek tragic actor. He is wearing huge boots called *cothurnus* which made him appear larger than life to the audience.

masks — bad characters wore evil-looking masks and good characters wore pleasant masks, for example.

All over the world, dressing up began as a form of either hunting, magic, religion or local **superstition**.

Throughout history many religions have used special costumes in ceremonies. This costume represents the god of *Teyyum* – a religion followed in a small area of southern India.

Costumes through the ages

Over the years, many different types of theatrical costume have been used. It is interesting to see how the styles and reasons for wearing particular costumes have hardly changed. In ancient Greece, for example, brightly patterned stage cloaks were worn by most of the actors. Sad characters would wear dark cloaks and happy characters wore colourful cloaks so the audience would recognize who was who.

In the sixteenth century, the Italians performed a type of theatre called *Commedia dell'Arte*. This was made up of characters who were well known for their amazing costumes. One of the characters, *Arlecchino* or *Harlequin*, is still popular all over the world. *Harlequin's* costume was originally made from patches of material but is now made of colourful, diamond-shaped pieces of silk.

William Shakespeare's plays were performed in the sixteenth century in very rich and colourful costumes against simple background scenery. The costumes were not always historically correct — in the play **Julius Caesar**, the leading character sometimes wore **Elizabethan** dress when he should have been dressed as a Roman, for example.

In the seventeenth century, actors and actresses wore costumes from countries all over

An actor wearing a harlequin's costume. The harlequin is a character from the sixteenth century *Commedia dell'Arte* theatre in Italy.

the world. By the eighteenth century, designers were paying more attention to the historical detail of the costumes and were not using masks quite so much.

It is only now in the twentieth century that theatrical costume is historically correct because designers have the resources and opportunities to research plays and discover what the proper costumes should be like.

Many of William Shakespeare's plays are performed in Elizabethan dress, as this was the era in which he wrote them. *King Lear* (above) was set in mythological (imaginary) England, but is performed here in Elizabethan dress.

Chapter 3
Around the World

All over the world people like to dress up. It is interesting to see how many of today's costumes have been influenced by the past. Costume follows tradition, fashion, trends, culture and budgets. Most countries have a famous type of drama or dance and many perform traditional folk legends each year at special national festivals or celebrations.

In England folk dancing is still popular, particularly Morris dancing. People can still be seen on special occasions dancing in groups in country villages. Originally the dance was to celebrate the coming of spring. Square dancing is still performed in some parts of the USA. This is a kind of folk dance where performers dress in checkered outfits and someone calls out the steps of the dance accompanied by music. Australian **Aborigines** perform an ancient ritual dance called *corroboree*. They dress up and act as birds and insects to show how close humans are to nature and the earth.

France is well known for its mime artists, perhaps the most famous being Marcel Marceau. Performers dress mostly in black and white and act out scenes without words.

At the carnival held each year in Port of Spain, Trinidad, people dress up in magnificent and colourful costumes as part of the celebrations.

A Native American dancer in New Mexico, USA.

Mime is a form of drama that uses actions and not words.

A scene from a Japanese *noh* play. *Noh* drama uses music, dancing, chanting and elaborate costumes and masks.

In Japan, *kabuki*, a type of dance drama, is based on tragic stories of love, revenge and death. The costumes used are heavily embroidered and brilliantly coloured. Masks are very popular in Chinese theatre, as are beautifully decorated and embroidered costumes.

In India a special kind of drama called *kathakali* is performed. This involves male

An extremely colourful and dramatic costume worn in Japanese theatre.

actors who dance to **epic** stories about ancient India. The facial expressions are important and each particular movement has an exact meaning. The actors wear thick, heavy make-up to give added expression to their faces.

These and many other folk legends and dance dramas still have their place in life today. In the theatre in any country, the costume depends mainly on the style of the play, the ideas of the producer and the costume designer. So, in one country alone, many different kinds and designs of theatrical costume may be used.

Above A performer from a Chinese opera. Imagine how long it must have taken to make her intricate head-dress. Also, notice how heavy make-up gives this performer a strikingly dramatic look.

Left The Bhutanese folk dancer is wearing a very evil-looking mask. Can you see the small skulls on it?

Chapter 4
Stage Costumes

Pantomime and circus

Pantomime is like comedy with a story to tell and is full of many interesting and funny characters. They are very popular in many countries, especially around Christmas. It is thought that pantomime first began in Italy, closely linked to *Commedia dell'Arte*. The characters are all larger than life and most of them wear costumes that are very **exaggerated** — extremely large stomachs,

Above A nasty-looking giant, Blundoor Boro, from the pantomime *Jack and the Beanstalk*. The way he stands and the prop he holds make him look even more sinister.

Left A male actor dressed and made-up to play an ugly sister in *Cinderella*. In pantomime males usually play female roles and vice versa. All the characters are larger than life.

Television and film costumes

Since the beginning of this century a new kind of theatre has become popular — the moving picture or film. Even within the last thirty years, yet another new form of theatre has taken people by storm — television. The introduction of these new media has led to lots of new ideas about theatrical costume.

In the theatre the audience can see the actor or actress's whole body so the costume must be correct from head to foot. For television a large amount of the filming is of the head and shoulders only. The television audience has the opportunity to look at a particular part of the actor or actress for, sometimes, a long period of time. Because of this the costume designer must make sure that all the costumes and accessories are correct in every detail. Similarly, in feature films where the camera concentrates on particular actors or actresses for a period of time, their costumes must be suitable and correct.

Costume designers must take great care when selecting colours for a television production. Some colours will give a 'strobe' effect, when the picture looks fuzzy to the audience as the colours interfere with the cameras and the lights.

Each time a play is performed in the theatre, the costumes can be changed if required. Once a film or television programme has been made, unless it is in period costume, it can soon look old-fashioned. For example, a film made only twenty years ago in **contemporary** costume looks very old-fashioned today.

Barry Humphries, the successful Australian 'superstar', in his two famous roles, Sir Les Patterson (above) and Dame Edna Everage (left).

pointes. The shoes have block toes and are made from satin and **hessian** which is baked in a heated oven to make it go stiff.

Modern ballet often depends on bright and unusual costumes to help tell the story. Romantic ballet is based on setting a mood and atmosphere. Classical ballet is more concerned with the sleek and sophisticated overall look of the dancers which is reflected in their costumes.

In classical ballet, dancers wear costumes that are specially designed to be light and give plenty of freedom of movement. Modern ballet costumes, however, are more important to the overall dramatic effect.

Ballet costumes

Ballet is a type of dance that is set to music without words. It is very important that the costumes and sets help the audience to understand the story.

Ballet dancers do not stop moving throughout a performance so there are some important points the designer must remember. Balance is essential to dancers so the costumes must be light and not weigh them down. The costumes rarely cover up the dancers' outlines because the shape adds to the beauty and skill of the dance.

Classical ballerinas wear tutus — frilly skirts which are made from a material called tarlatan. Tutus are very short because it is difficult for dancers to perform in long skirts.

Ballet dancers are trained to dance on the tips of their toes from the age of about thirteen. They wear special ballet shoes called

Above **Classical ballet dancers wearing a traditional tutu (female) and leotard and tights (male).**

Left **A ballet dancer playing Jeremy Fisher in** *Tales of Beatrix Potter.* **Imagine how difficult it must be to leap about and dance in a frog costume.**

long, pointed noses, huge feet and padded shoulders, for example. There are many popular pantomimes including *Jack and the Beanstalk*, *Cinderella* with her ugly sisters, *Aladdin* with Widow Twankey and *Puss in Boots*.

In most pantomimes there are a number of traditional characters: the 'Dame' is a female character played by a male dressed as a woman. The costume is always bright and bold, often with an outrageous wig and a huge, false beauty spot. The leading male character is usually played by a female wearing a tunic and leggings. All the costumes are designed to catch the audience's eye. They are made using sequins, feathers, bows, satin, patchwork and often outrageous wigs.

The circus is made up of many interesting characters. The person who introduces the various acts traditionally wears a top hat or tails to show that he or she is in command. The trapeze artists wear tight-fitting outfits made of a shiny, glittery material which shows off their **agile** movements. It is hard to imagine a circus without clowns. Clowns use heavy stage make-up to make themselves look happy or sad. They often dress in odd pieces of clothing with large buttons and baggy trousers. Their dress is extremely funny and is an important part of the overall comedy of their act.

The many funny and sad faces of the circus clown. It is interesting to see how the same make-up can be used to give different results.

Above Actor Christopher Lee in the horror film *The House of Long Shadows*. Notice how special effects blood and the choice of costume – a dark jacket that looks sinister and a white shirt that shows up the blood – create an impression of what his character must be.

Right The actor on the left is wearing a special ape's costume for the film *Greystoke*, about the life of Tarzan. The costume is very realistic right down to the last detail.

Chapter 5
Famous Costumes

Many costumes have been designed in such a way that it does not matter which actor or actress plays the part, the audience will still recognize the character. These costumes are often made with a lighthearted approach — for example, Superman or Supergirl, the Tin Man in the *Wizard of Oz* or Batman. In recent years new theatre productions have involved dressing actors and actresses as cats in *Cats* and performing a whole musical on roller skates in *Starlight Express*. Fun musicals seem to appeal to people of all ages.

There are many different international characters that can be identified purely by their costumes. For example, Groucho Marx

Above **Superman is pictured here flying above the New York skyline with Lois Lane.**

Left **Costume and make-up have been used to great effect in the successful stage musical *Cats*.**

A scene from the stage production of *The Wizard of Oz*. From left to right: the Tin Man, Dorothy, the Cowardly Lion, the Straw Man and Toto the dog.

with his famous fat cigar and bushy moustache; Charlie Chaplin with his cane and hat; Laurel and Hardy — very thin and very fat; and one of the most famous clowns of all, Oleg Popov with his checked hat, floppy bow tie and big red nose.

In the production of a serious or dramatic play the costumes require lots of research to make sure they are historically correct down to the last detail. Musicals and comedies, on the other hand, require lots of imagination and a sense of fun to make them interesting, amusing and original.

Minnie and Mickey Mouse, characters that are seen on television, in films and in magazines all over the world, are pictured here at Disneyworld in Florida, USA. The life-size costumes look very effective.

Chapter 6
The Make-Up Artist

Make-up is an important part of theatre. It adds the finishing touches to any costume. If an actor or actress is dressed up as an old person, make-up can make his or her face look old. Stage lights in any theatre are strong and bright and make the performers' faces look pale. By wearing make-up their faces will look normal under the lights.

The make-up artist's job is very important, as he or she has to change the faces of actors and actresses to suit the part they are playing. They do this by using theatrical make-up.

There are three different types of foundation make-up that act as a base — greasepaint, cream or pancake and a matt solution. A cold cream is usually put on before pancake foundation as it is very thick and likely to go blotchy. Cream or grease

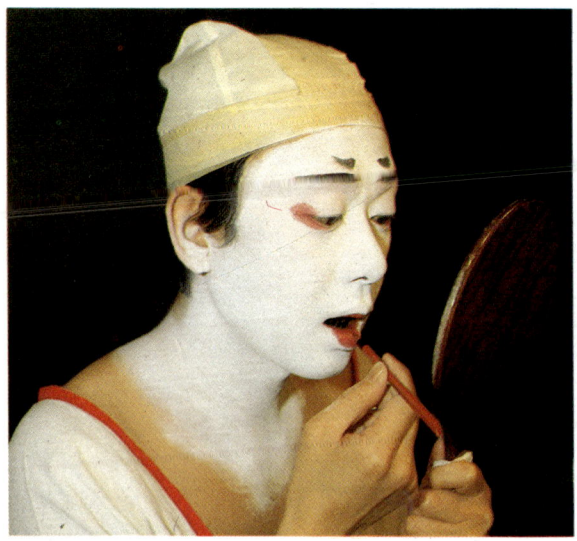

Below This Japanese *kabuki* actor is applying special make-up — bright red lipstick to emphasize his lips, red shadow on the corners of his eyes and black kohl on his eyebrows to give a dramatic effect. This make-up makes his features stand out under the heavy glare of the stage lights.

Left A Japanese *kabuki* actor puts on a thick matt foundation that acts as a flawless base for the rest of his make-up.

foundation can be applied straight on to the skin. They come in different shades so the wearer can choose whichever one suits their particular needs.

The most expressive feature of the face is the eyes. They need special attention so the whole audience can see them clearly. A selection of black and brown eye liners, mascara and dark eye shadows is essential. Rouge is applied to the lips and cheeks to give them colour and the whole face is finished off with powder that seals the make-up. The powder is a **neutral** colour so it does not change the colour of the make-up. Liquid make-up is put on the body with a sponge.

Nose putty is used to change the shape of parts of the actor or actress's face. The putty is moulded to the required shape and pressed on to the face. Black tooth wax can be lodged into the cracks of the teeth to give the appearance of missing teeth. Hair can be changed by using wigs, often made of natural hair.

Special effects make-up artist, Rick Baker, prepares an actor for his role in the spoof horror film *An American Werewolf in London*.

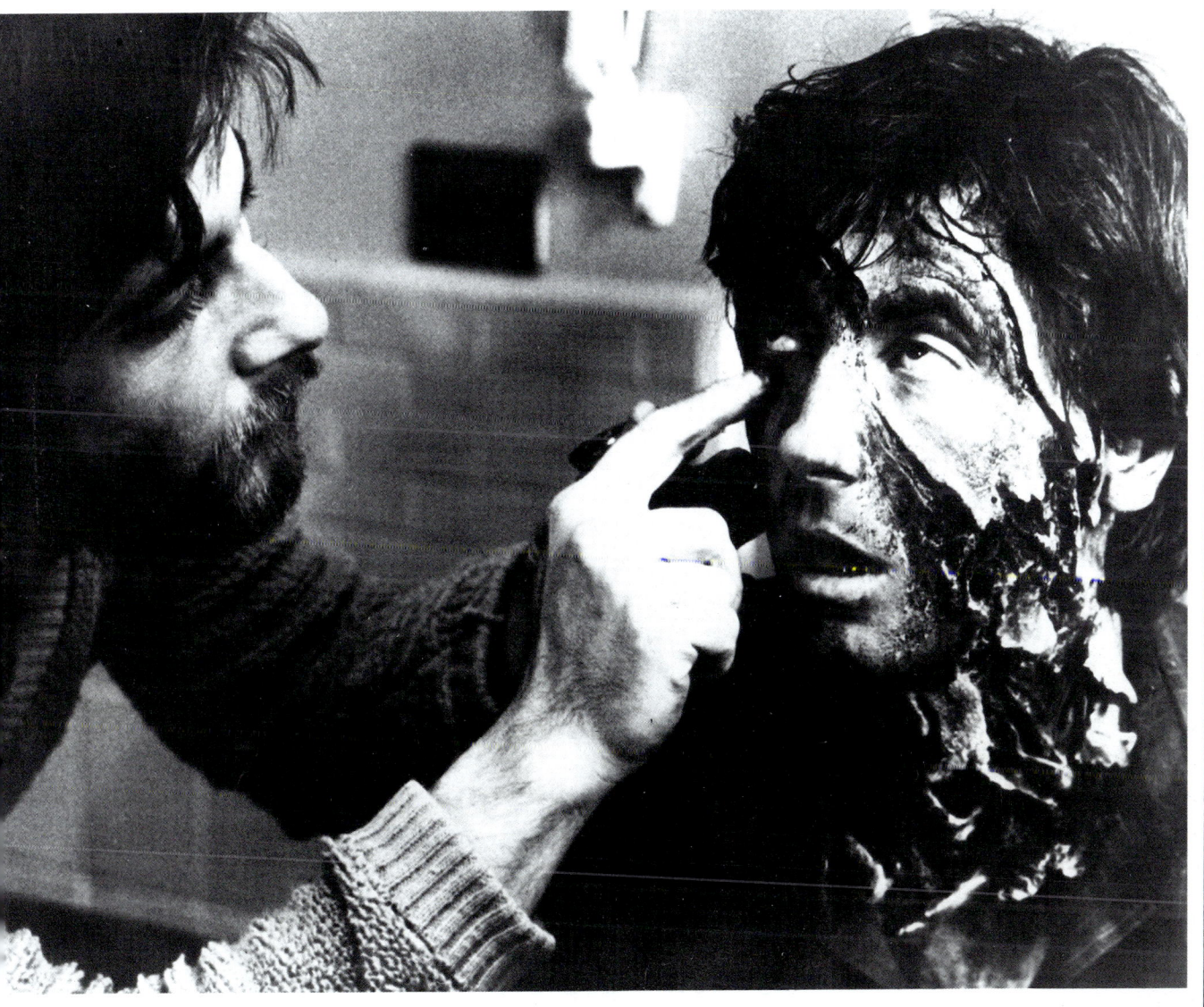

Chapter 7

Masks and Props

Many types of very early theatre involved the use of masks — ancient Greek theatre and the *Commedia dell'Arte,* for example. Masks are still used today and unlike make-up, which cannot change the bone structure of the face, masks can make actors and actresses look completely different.

Masks can be made from **papier mâché** and styled over a clay model head. This produces a stiff mask which can be decorated with items such as feathers, beads and false

An assortment of brightly coloured and decorated masks made by school children.

hair. Rubber **latex** is also used to make masks by pouring liquid latex into a plastic mould. This produces a mask which is soft and flexible and fits close to the skin. The finished mask can be decorated to suit the character. Masks can also be easily made from paper.

All moveable items except lighting and equipment, scenery and costumes are called props. There are different types of props: set or scene props — large items such as furniture or plants; dressing props — curtains, lamps or pictures; **rehearsal** props — used during rehearsals instead of real props; hand or action props — small items used by the actor such as food, drinks or books. It is essential that these items fit in with the overall costume and that an exact list of everything is made up so nothing is forgotten.

To make a paper mask you need:
1 sheet of paper 209mm × 296mm, crayons, scissors, string and glue.
Remember that scissors can be very sharp, so ask an adult to help you when using them.

1. Hold the paper to your face and gently outline your features with a pencil. You may need to ask a friend to help you with this.

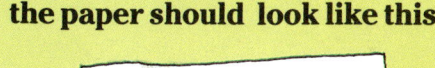
the paper should look like this

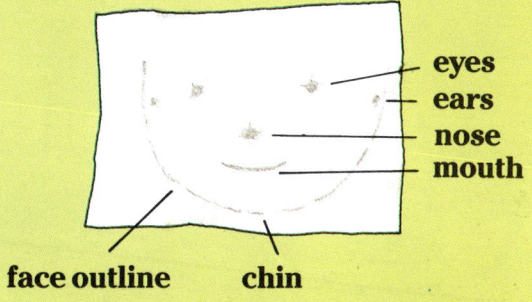
face outline   chin
eyes
ears
nose
mouth

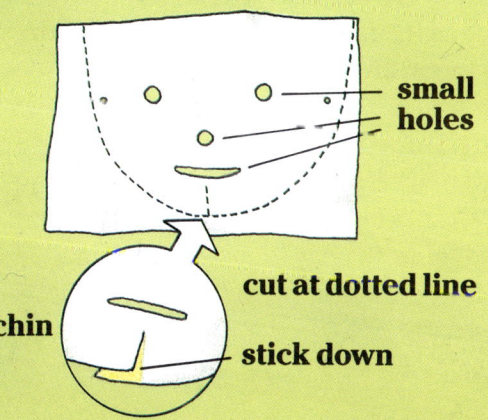
small holes
cut at dotted line
stick down
chin

2. Cut out the holes where the eyes, nose and mouth marks were made. Where the chin mark is, snip the paper, make a small fold and glue together. This makes the mask fold to the shape of your face. Make a small hole where the ear marks are and thread some string through to enable the mask to be fastened at the back. From the ears to the chin cut an oval shape to follow the outline of your face.

3. When this is finished, try the pattern of the mask on. If the mask fits it is then ready to be coloured in. This mask shows a happy person. You can make the mask look like anyone or anything you wish.

25

Chapter 8

Making Costumes

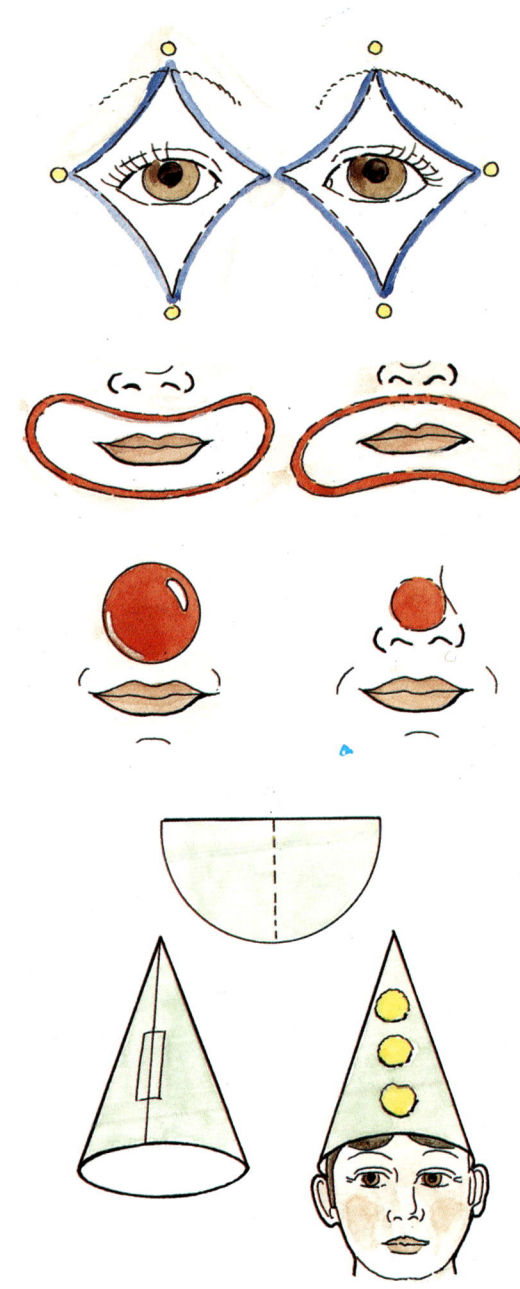

How to make a clown outfit

Some costumes can be made easily from everyday articles that can be found in the home. Simple accessories can be bought from most toy shops, for example, face paint. Clothes can be obtained from adults, but do not forget to ask permission first.
You will need: face paints, cardboard, cotton wool, glue, paints, old shirt and baggy trousers, braces, large shoes, crepe paper.

1. Make-up

a. Eyes can be made up into different shapes. One of the most popular designs is to draw a diamond around each eye and outline it with a darker colour.
b. The mouth can be made to look happy or sad. Red make-up is the best as it stands out well.
c. The nose can be either false, which can be bought from a toy or joke shop. A blob of face paint (red) on the tip of the nose can look just as good.

2. The hat

A fun hat can be made from cardboard, crayons, cotton wool and glue.
a. Cut a semi circle of card.
b. Fold around the head and stick (a) to (b) to ensure a secure fit. Cotton wool balls can be stuck onto the hat to give a pom-pom effect. Alternatively the hat can be coloured in with crayons.

3. The hair
Hair can be made from crepe paper, thinly shredded and stuck to the back of the hat.

4. The finale
Dress in an old shirt, baggy trousers with braces and a large pair of shoes.

How to make a pantomime cat

You will need: a paper bag (NOT plastic), crayons, leotard, gloves, tights and one stocking – preferably black. Pipe cleaners, glue, cotton, needle, old rag.

1. The mask
Ensure that the paper bag will fit over your head and gently outline your features with a pencil. Cut out holes where the marks were made. In each corner (a) and (b) of the bag put a spot of glue and pinch them together so they look like pointed cats ears.
Paint the cat's face on the front of the bag. Thread the pipe cleaners through the nose to give the impression of cats whiskers.

2. The tail
Take one black stocking and fill it with old rags so it looks like a long sausage. This is your tail which you can sew on to the leotard at the base of your back. If you want the tail to move with you, you can tie a piece of string to the end of the tail and then loop it around your wrist. The tail will then move when you want it to.

3. The body
The black leotard, tights and gloves will give the impression of a slinky cat, ready to pounce.

Remember to have an adult present and to be very careful indeed when using scissors.

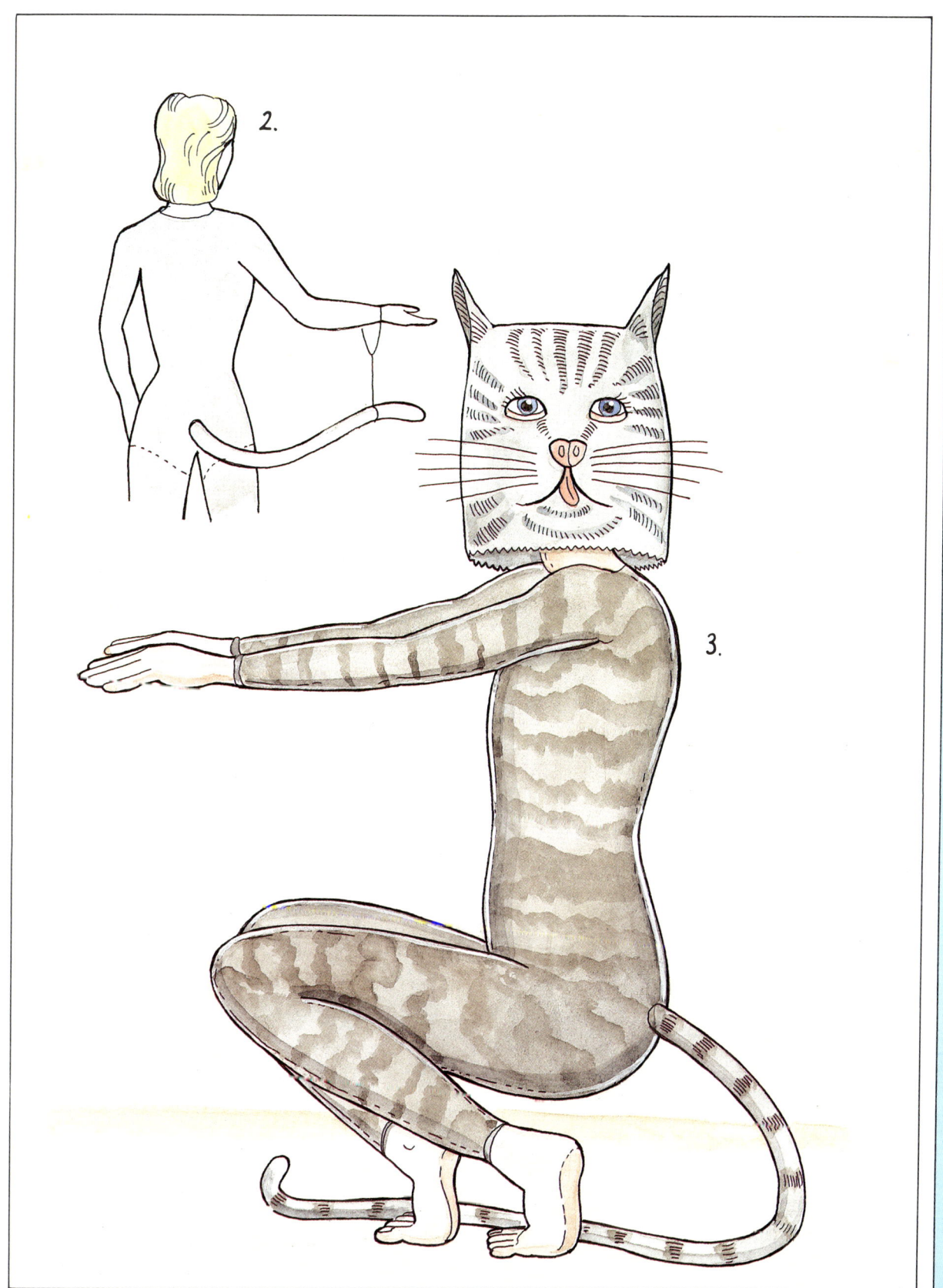

Glossary

Aborigines The original inhabitants of any country. Today, the term refers specifically to the original inhabitants of Australia.
Agile Lively and active.
Contemporary Something which is of a particular time.
Elizabethan Related to the period of English history between 1558 and 1603 when Elizabeth I was queen.
Epic A very long poem about heroic deeds.
Exaggerated Larger than life.
Expression The look on someone's face.
Hessian A strong, rough cloth often used to make sacks.
Julius Caesar the famous Roman general, statesperson and historian who ruled between 100 and 44 BC. Shakespeare wrote a play about his life.
Latex A milky fluid which is produced from the rubber tree and is used to make rubber.
Neutral Having no colour.
Papier mâché A substance made of paper pulp which is sometimes mixed with glue and other materials. It is used when wet to make things like models or boxes which become hard and strong when dry.
Period costumes Costumes which come from a particular time in history.
Prehistoric The time before history was written and records were kept.
Producer The person responsible for making a play, film or programme. His or her duties involve preparing the actors and actresses, deciding how the script should be dealt with and the overall design.
Realistic True to life.
Rehearsal The private practice before the public performance.
Set The scenery that is used for a play or film.
Superstition A thought or belief that is not real and that is not backed by fact.
Vivid Bright and dazzling.

Books to read

If you would like to find out more about theatrical costume, you might like to read the following books:

Dance by Eleanor Van Zandt (Wayland, 1988)
Making Costumes for Plays by Joan Peters and Anna Sutcliffe (Batsford, 1985)
Theatre by Howard Loxton (Wayland, 1988)

Reference
All the World's a Stage by Ronald Harwood (Methuen, 1984)
Costume in the Theatre by James Laver (Harrap, 1984)

Index

Actors 4, 5, 6, 8, 13, 22, 24, 25
Aladdin 15
Ancient Greeks 6, 8, 24
Audience 4, 5, 8, 15, 16, 18, 20
Australia 10

Ballet 16-17
Batman 20

Cagney, James **5**
Cats 20
Cave paintings 6
Characters 6, 14
   angry 5
   bad 7
   evil 4
   happy 8
   noisy 4
   sad 8
Chaplin, Charlie 21
Chinese theatre 12
Cinderella 15
Circus 14-15
Clowns 15, 21
Comedy 14, 15, 21
Costumes
   around the world 8-9, 10-13
   ballet 16-17
   Elizabethan 8
   film 4, 18-19
   fun and famous 20-21
   historical 6-9
   pantomime 15
   period 5, 18
   stage 14-19
   television 4, 18-19
   theatrical 4, 8, 13

Dance 6, 10, 13
   ballet 16
   corroboree 10
   folk 10
Designers 5, 9, 13, 16, 18
Disneyworld **21**
Drama 10, 12
Dressing up 4-5, 10
   as a disguise 6

Everage, Dame Edna **18**
Expression 5, 13

Fashion 10
Films 18-19
Folk legends 10, 13
Foundation make-up 22

Greasepaint 22
Greek theatre **7**

Harlequin 8

India 12, 13

Jack and the Beanstalk **14**, 15
Japanese theatre **5**

Kabuki 12, **22**
Kathakali 12
King Lear **9**

Laurel and Hardy 21
Leggings 15

Magazines 5
Magic 7
Make-up 4, 5, 13, 15, 22-3, 24
Make-up artist 22-3
Making costumes
   a clown outfit 26-7
   a pantomime cat 28-9
   masks 25
Marcel Marceau 10
Masks 4, 5, 6, 7, 9, 12, 24-5
Materials 4, 8, 17
Mickey Mouse **21**
Mime 10, **11**
Museums 5
Music 16, 21

National festivals 10
Noh drama **11**
Nose putty 23

Pantomime **4**, 14-15
Papier mâché 24
Patterson, Sir Les **18**
Pointes 17
Popov, Oleg 21
Producer 5, 13
Props 24-5
Puss in Boots 15

Rehearsal 25
Religion 7
Rouge 23

Scenery 8, 25
Set 4
Set designer 5
Special effects **23**
Stage costumes 14-19
Stage lights 22, 25
Starlight Express 20
Supergirl 20
Superman 20
Superstition 7

Tales of Beatrix Potter **16**
Television 18-19
Tooth wax 23
Trapeze artists 15
Tunic 15
Tutus 17

USA 10, **11**

Wizard of Oz 20, **21**

31

Index

Actors 4, 5, 6, 8, 13, 22, 24, 25
Aladdin 15
Ancient Greeks 6, 8, 24
Audience 4, 5, 8, 15, 16, 18, 20
Australia 10

Ballet 16-17
Batman 20

Cagney, James **5**
Cats 20
Cave paintings 6
Characters 6, 14
   angry 5
   bad 7
   evil 4
   happy 8
   noisy 4
   sad 8
Chaplin, Charlie 21
Chinese theatre 12
Cinderella 15
Circus 14-15
Clowns 15, 21
Comedy 14, 15, 21
Costumes
   around the world 8-9, 10-13
   ballet 16-17
   Elizabethan 8
   film 4, 18-19
   fun and famous 20-21
   historical 6-9
   pantomime 15
   period 5, 18
   stage 14-19
   television 4, 18-19
   theatrical 4, 8, 13

Dance 6, 10, 13
   ballet 16
   corroboree 10
   folk 10
Designers 5, 9, 13, 16, 18
Disneyworld **21**
Drama 10, 12
Dressing up 4-5, 10

   as a disguise 6

Everage, Dame Edna **18**
Expression 5, 13

Fashion 10
Films 18-19
Folk legends 10, 13
Foundation make-up 22

Greasepaint 22
Greek theatre **7**

Harlequin 8

India 12, 13

Jack and the Beanstalk **14**, 15
Japanese theatre **5**

Kabuki 12, **22**
Kathakali 12
King Lear **9**

Laurel and Hardy 21
Leggings 15

Magazines 5
Magic 7
Make-up 4, 5, 13, 15, 22-3, 24
Make-up artist 22-3
Making costumes
   a clown outfit 26-7
   a pantomime cat 28-9
   masks 25
Marcel Marceau 10
Masks 4, 5, 6, 7, 9, 12, 24-5
Materials 4, 8, 17
Mickey Mouse **21**
Mime 10, **11**
Museums 5
Music 16, 21

National festivals 10
Noh drama **11**
Nose putty 23

Pantomime **4**, 14-15
Papier mâché 24
Patterson, Sir Les **18**
Pointes 17
Popov, Oleg 21
Producer 5, 13
Props 24-5
Puss in Boots 15

Rehearsal 25
Religion 7
Rouge 23

Scenery 8, 25
Set 4
Set designer 5
Special effects **23**
Stage costumes 14-19
Stage lights 22, 25
Starlight Express 20
Supergirl 20
Superman 20
Superstition 7

Tales of Beatrix Potter **16**
Television 18-19
Tooth wax 23
Trapeze artists 15
Tunic 15
Tutus 17

USA 10, **11**

Wizard of Oz 20, **21**

Picture acknowledgements

The Publisher would like to thank the following for supplying the pictures used in this book: Bryan and Cherry Alexander 11 (top left); Aquarius Picture Library 5 (top), 19, 23; BBC Enterprises 18; Chapel Studios 4 (left), 5 (bottom), 10, 11 (top right), 11 (bottom), 16 (bottom); Mary Evans Picture Library 6, 7 (left), 8; Hutchison Library 7 (right), 12, 13, 22 (both); National Film Archive 16 (top); Photostage 20 (left), 21 (top); Topham Picture Library 4 (right), 9, 14, 15, 17, 20 (right), 24; Malcolm Walker 25; Wayland Picture Library 21 (bottom); Stephen Wheele 26-7, 28-9.